SLOW ASCENT

For Pearl who inspires.

Acknowledgements:

Some of these poems have appeared in *The Windsor Review*, and the anthology: *Smaller Than God*.

I also wish to thank the following writers for their support and inspiration: Roo Borson, Marty Gervais, Shirley Graham, Don Domanski, Kim Maltman, Christopher Wiseman, Don Coles, Marilyn Bowering, Barry Dempster, Ken Rivard, Fred Stenson, Stephen Guppy, Bruce Hunter, Mona Fertig, and Pamela Banting. And my friends on Salt Spring Island and in Calgary.

Special thanks to Peter Levitt and John B. Lee for their inspiration and editorial assistance.

Contents

50 Varieties of Apples

50 Varieties of Apples 11
The Shores of the Salish Sea 12
Half Life of Love 14
Fine Porcelain Cannot be Mended 15
Hush 16
The Culls 17

Slow Ascent

Slow Ascent 21
No Complaint 23
Coming Up Short 26
Man of Happiness/Man of Sorrow 28

Rendition

Rendition 31
Playing for Keeps 33
72 Virgins 37

Live Current

Attention 41
Unaware 32
Winter Weight 44
Liftoff 46
Wet Nurse 48
God Must Have 49
Startled 50
Following the Sound 52
Overlap 53

My Empire of Dirt

The 8 Known Photographs of Arthur Rimbaud 57
The Worth of Fathers 59
Two of Everything 60
This Shiver 61
Adam's Rib 62
Oh God, all your orators speak gibberish 63

50 Varieties of Apples

50 Varieties of Apples
For Pearl

Fat, King apples ripen
on trees facing Long Harbour Road.
50 varieties grow on Salt Spring
and each fall
they redden leafless branches.
Yesterday we lay in bed reading,
your slender fingers
traveled my body
and for a time we let go.
Like those autumn apples
we surrendered
to this uneven passing of summer.

I focused on your fingers
tried to anticipate their path
but I guessed wrong.
Yet that is love, too,
always guessing
what the other will do next
finding worthiness in that one riddle.

Today the sight of those
near-ripe apples reminds me
how their ripening
measures the year
in weather and light,
and how the earth remembers,
each hour shed
of memory and time.
Even as I hold them
their flesh grows
brown in my hand.

The Shores of the Salish Sea

Each year along the shores
Of the Salish Sea
I watch the wind-stirred ocean
And see that
What comes and goes in us
Comes and goes in all that surrounds.
I want to stand firm
Where sleeping is easy
Amongst trees grown abundant with light.

Around our house
They sway to a Southeasterly
Pushing inland off the Salish Sea
With a thrust that
All but the arbutus give in to.
Their contorted trunks
Spread wide
Resist such a wind
As skin-smooth trunks
Contort and lean away from the water.

What must it be like to be
That bound to the earth?

I feel I've lived
Here long enough
To claim these shores
As my home.
I've put down stubborn roots
Even the strongest
Winter storms can't
Pry loose.
Home is the piece of earth

That serves us
Where we stop for a moment
To say *Ah*.
I take a long inhale
And sense it here
A holding in place
A longing to winter well.

Half Life of Love

On the road into Ganges
I pass a couple with a dog
Talking to another couple with a dog
And wonder what they are discussing.

Our own dog, Emily,
Sleeps cuddled next to you
Or at your feet as you work at the computer
And I am astounded by how
Dogs love more deeply
And yet they too forget
Abandon or shift their affection.
When you are out of town
At first, Emily closes in on herself
Barely leaves her bed except to eat
And then she only nibbles.
Most of the time, she curls into a ball and waits
And waits and waits
For the sound of your key in the door.
But if you are away for several days
She lets go that hurt
Stands outside my office
For a time considering her options
Before she crosses the threshold and lies down.

Fine Porcelain Cannot be Mended:
An apology

When I reach home I find you working. You stop as I tell you about a dairy truck getting stuck half on and off the ferry. No matter how the driver rocked his truck it would not budge. The vehicles had been jammed on board so tightly, I worried we'd be trapped until morning. In the end they brought a tow truck from town to winch the truck out of the way. You smiled when I finished the story and started typing immediately and I was amazed that you could take up so quickly where you had left off. It was then I realized I'd thought only of my words and how important they were and hadn't given consideration to what you had been writing when I barged in. Later you read me your day's work and I listened for some sign of my intrusion, but your writing flowed naturally as though I hadn't interrupted.

Hush
For Pearl

I feel
The hush, hush from
Nowhere
If time weren't so perfect
So cruel
If only there was a seam
To slip through back to
Earlier in the day
When I could do no wrong
Even made you laugh.
Your mouth so kissable.

I bang onto walls
In this incessant *Now*.
The present wrongly constructed
From what the past demands.

Tonight, lying alone in bed
I think of you in yours
Love viewed from afar
Today we fought
And everything went badly
And I learn again
The easy damage of anger.

A neighbour's dog barks.
My fingers drum the sheets.
You are not here.
My dreams
The hush, hush of
Nowhere.

The Culls
For Pearl

Below us Fulford Valley ripened
In late autumn light as
Rain-heavy clouds dispersed
Above a small flock of sheep.
From a distance their bowed heads
Appeared as if joined to the ground.
There is only our forward movement.
The hills remain fixed
Only what inhabits them changing.
On your electric bike, you clocked
70 kilometers per hour down Lee's Hill.
The air smoothed our skin
And you pumped your legs with such strength
I loved you then as I did later at your brother's funeral.

When we returned home from our bike ride,
Your nephew called with the news
Of Dave's car accident.
Your brother never saw the approaching lights.
He survived for a week on life support
And when he was eventually taken off
He lasted longer than expected.
When the call finally came you sobbed
And grief moved through you
With a new set of surprises.
Those we love are culled one at a time.

When we returned to Salt Spring
After Dave's funeral
Sheep no longer covered
The freshly harvested hillside.

I thought back to that day on our bikes
Before all the grief
And if I could pick a moment
When you looked completely alive
It would be that one.
It wasn't the speed you traveled
Or the exhilaration of beating the traffic
But the prized absence of words
And how your bike
Barely touched the ground.

Slow Ascent

A Slow Ascent

I study a photograph from 1940
Uncertain if the man is my father
Because a shadow covers his face.
But I immediately recognize his hands
Crossed at the wrist and supporting a propped shotgun.
It's a photo taken to prove he'd killed something.
But it's his hands that matter now.

He hunted often as a young man
And years later told me
How he loved the slow ascent
Of a flock of mallards over Longbow Lake
Their wings gripping air solid as ground
As they lifted, like fingers the edge of a cliff.
He tracked their progress with his shotgun
Until they were fully in flight
Then he shot one of the stragglers.
That bird, heavy and earth bound,
Dropped so quickly
My father barely had time
To send the dog
Who luckily knew exactly
Where to go.

In the photo, he leans back
Maybe a little afraid of all that happens next.
I know most of that now
Could tell him what to watch out for
But that might nudge him
Away from me altogether.
He has been dead these ten years.
But seeing that photograph brings back the pain.

The dead leave so little behind
To be glimpsed only here and there
Until that too is gone.

I remember how near the end of his life
His hands started to shake
And I would try to steady them
But as soon as I took mine away
His began shaking again.
"Never mind," he'd say,
"I've gotten used to it."
And then he would light a cigarette
And for that brief moment
While he held the lighter
Against the tip
His hands went still.

No Complaint

My mother returns now in old age
to the girl she was
when she stood
at the edge of a small lake
with a few fish,
frogs, and snakes
nothing God couldn't take back
if he wanted to.
He didn't speak to her
didn't touch her hand
or point out across the lake
to the other shore
where a few boats had gathered
seeking shelter.
He waded into the water
until he was up to his neck
and motioned for her to follow,
but she remained steadfast
her toes clinging to the last bit
of earth afforded her.
God waved again but this time
to say *suit yourself*
and dove under.
He never resurfaced
nor were the boats on the far shore
disturbed in the slightest.

My mother stood there a long time
without moving
sometimes I think she is standing there still
not sure why she didn't enter the water,
not sure why she hasn't stepped back.

She's seventy-eight
drinks beer with a boyfriend.
There is much ordinariness in her life
much that is no longer remembered
that happened once and there were words
for it but it's gone now
closed away like God that day
the water sealing over him
as it does with deep diving harp seals.
Without my father
she hasn't changed.
She still talks about God often
but he's not really there anymore
not in the way he was before
when her children still ran around the house
making more chores.

She has no complaints really
no regrets that she's ever put into words
although I can imagine some:
the lack of money,
the bad turns,
my father's excesses.
From the living room window of her suite
she can see downtown Winnipeg,
describes the lights to me sometimes on the phone
as if they weren't there the week before
or before that
just like God wasn't there and then he was
and then he wasn't.

Though she once played the piano
she doesn't now.
Sometimes, she spreads her fingers

to show the chords.
She has a simple life with few bills
a life I envy especially on those days
I step outside and can't remember
where I'm going.
She's mentioned to me numerous times
that day at the lake with God
each time she describes it a little differently
and never mentions God being there
That's the part I knew without her telling me.
I understand why God
went under the water that day.

When I visit my mother she makes
me tea although she sometimes forgets
where things are.
Once I look under her pillow
and find dozens of bunched up tissues.
She says she takes one to bed with her every night.
Funny she remembers to do that but not
to remove them in the morning.
She tells me she prays for me every day
and asks if I do the same for her.
I say I do although usually I don't.
How many lies has she told me?
There aren't such answers.
I know my mother's days on the earth
are not many and each time we speak
a little more of what once was disappears.
What choices do the living have?
Like the God of my mother's youth,
Perhaps we simply slip beneath the surface
one day and vanish.

Coming Up Short
For Amanda Richard

Amanda fell from the feather ledge of life. Leukemia took her, my brother's daughter, at 21, a new mother. The world is damn cold at times. At the end she lay in silence, surrounded by quiet, feeling the wordless panic of dying young.

Every day my brother drove to the Health Sciences Building knowing, yet not wanting to know. He parked in the same lot as the day before, perhaps next to the same blue Volkswagen. The same hundred odd steps to her room. The tubes bleeding into her joining her more to another world than this one. Her eyes, her face aged by chemotherapy, by the wounding.

Then near the end seeing the life leave her, as her insides bled. The panic she knew and there were no words. Not a single one that mattered when most needed, when she got this close. They all come up short, except to fill the need to not let it all be silence. He fought back the tears every day, smiled for her, and told her jokes, but even laughter has no power against this. The days wasted by the gathering. Our bodies follow an incline plane and we are on the outside only what our insides manage.

My brother stood at her gravesite as my nephew shielded the container of her ashes from the wind off Lake Winnipeg—brisk and eternal at their backs. Out on the lake gulls swooped, clipped the water, and lifted again. Along the shore the grass bristled. This is a busy place to leave her. My brother remained at the graveside longest. His usual noisy kidding silenced by that small patch of earth. He looked awkward in his suit, his hands crossed behind his back as if praying, although he has never prayed.

Near the end Amanda asked him why God disliked her so much, why her? He didn't have an answer and he'd asked the same question, of himself, of me, of everyone he could, but the only answer is that wind off the lake, icy even in August, but that's as certain as any of us will get. That and Amanda buried in her twenty-first year. The world no longer the prize it once was.

Amanda's bedroom had been across the hall from her parent's and when she was sick she slept there a few nights. To my brother, Amanda's sounds behind the door were no longer confirming, growing up noises, but the sounds of someone dying. Now her daughter, Keanna, occupies the same room and time sweeps away so much even memories are paper thin with little written on them. Sometimes when my brother opens the door in the morning he expects Amanda but finds Keanna instead.

Nothing is in its rightful place.

Man of Happiness/Man of Sorrow

My father woke that morning,
The same time as usual
Went to the bathroom.
On the way back to bed
He paused to look out
The hospital window
As the Winnipeg street
Filled with rush hour traffic.
Did he crave a cigarette—
his constant companion?
He sat on the edge of the bed
For a few minutes.
Did he look at his knees?
Were they shaking?
He blew his nose.
Coughed.
Then lay down,
Pulled the covers over him,
Closed his eyes,
Went to sleep.
Failed to wake.

Rendition

Rendition

"Amnesty International has reported that nearly 1,000 flights have been directly linked to the CIA through "front" companies, most of which, it says, have used European airspace. These "Rendition Flights" carry detainees to secret "black site" prisons in Eastern Europe or Central Asia, where the detainees are then tortured. A further 600 CIA flights were made by planes hired from US aviation companies." – The Guardian

A prisoner is strapped to a board
And submerged in water.
Whose hands lower
And lift this victim?
Ringless or ringed fingers
Folded in a lap?
How many have died
Been made to disappear
Names taken off lists
Livers removed and laid on a table?
We are all strangers
Whole rooms of us
Staring at screens
Asking questions
Flat stomachs or rounded
Does it matter?
I don't blame the pilots
Of those *Rendition* flights
Nor those who guard the prisoners
Sprinkled throughout the cabin.
Men with their heads bent
Perhaps even hooded
Do the pilots step from the plane

And quickly grab a coffee?
Chit chat to the ground crew?
All of this so routine
The mind numbs to it.
Evil does not enter or occupy.
Evil lingers like a scent.

In the mornings I wake
To a placid Salish Sea
Where a fishing boat
Or sloop cuts the water
With little more
Than a ripple
And I hear only the slightest
Huff, Huff of a breeze.
I can retreat to my computer
And type a poem
Or search the internet for news
Of the unraveling of the world.
I am free to pretend I am not connected
To the cruel, unjustified deeds of others.
We are a shattered, crumbling people
Lost in starlight.
Put us all out to sea
Cast us adrift
Do not pause to say goodbye
Be rid of us as quickly as possible
Because we are hell bound,
Oh so determinedly hell bound,
And that gathering shadow behind us
Is another rendition flight
None of them ever touches down.

Playing for Keeps
(Four years now in Iraq)

It's the parents of the American soldiers
In Iraq that I don't get
How they can allow their children to go?
Don't they know it's the future
They are giving up on?
I fear most
Those that believe in omnipresent evil
See it everywhere
Even on the face of the grocer
Down the street
The same stooped man
Who handles their oranges each morning
That man, that very man
Could topple buildings
Set fires under bridges, cars
Listen at his door
In the evening
What exactly is he saying to his wife
To his son?
The creaks in the floorboards
At night could be anything
Could be an old man's disturbed sleep
Or a plan
Which is it?
Send your sons and daughters to find out
And when they don't come back
Mourn them
Put up statues, shrines
That you visit daily, weekly, or monthly.

Once your children poked fingers
Through the rails of their cribs
And looked at you as though
You were all the good
The world could give them
And now where are they?
Gathered again in the dutiful earth
What's given up doesn't come back.
How did they sleep in their cribs?
Did they call out to you at night
Until you pushed away covers
And went to them, held them
In the warm sweep of late night
Promised them anything
If they'd only go
Back to sleep?
Perhaps you sang to them
Planted a kiss on infant cheeks.
Most thought of you as they died
Even pictured your face as it would look
The moment you got the news.

What can be said about lives
Laid down for such a cause?
No one will look back fondly
What was this war for?
Death is not uniquely human
Nor is dying for a cause
But foolish death is.

If I told you to shoot the man
Across the street peering into a shop window
Perhaps pondering a gift for his wife
Would you?

Why, then, is his life more valuable
Than your own child's?
The pain you feel
The tears you shed
What good are they?
This is a grieving time
And children are asked
To fight their parents' wars
History is a locked room
No one yet has been able to open.

What of the grocer?
Each night he counts the meager banknotes
From the day's sales
Counts them twice to be certain
It's never a large stack
But he shoves it into a bag for the night deposit
One night he is held up along the usual route
A young man with a pistol
Pulls the trigger
Perhaps even by mistake
But he leaves the grocer to die.

You send your children
To the streets of Baghdad
Where that grocer lived
And where he died
His money bag lay empty.
Don't blame him.
It's too late for blame now.
Think instead of those nights
You stayed awake while your child
Suffered through a fever
Think of the mornings

Their perky faces woke you
Think of the evenings in the park
All of that for the sake of a uniform
Then think of that old man
In his grocery shop
Your enemy
He had children too
Several sons worked with him in the shop
Until they were blown up
By a car bomb
He stood at their gravesides
He did not cry
It was as though they died in a car accident.
Like you he stayed at the graveside
A very long time
Asking questions of God
Expecting answers
For how else can all this be explained?
But God has nothing to do with it
It is all our own doing.

72 Virgins

A promise is easily broken
And yet men die for the promise
Of 72 virgins in the afterlife.
But they are really dying for
The quiet in their heads.

We are divided by our God.
Ruined by belief
Each of us a product of
The swollen, bitter earth.
It slips through our fingers
And we are buried in it
Returned to all that clay.
The earth goes on circling the sun
Spinning through space so exactly
Clocks can be set to it.
But look for God elsewhere.
What's God in us
Is not God in other creatures
Not even God in God
What is God in us
Promises 72 virgins because
Such promises are never binding.

Close your eyes at night
And listen to the whispers
They are all you have.
Try to make a God out of that.
But God is a kite uselessly
Caught in the branches of a dying tree.
All *that* God is good at
Is keeping an almighty distance.

Live Current

Attention

No breeze disturbs the trees tonight.
As I walk amongst their darkened shapes
Their lifeless poses mask a busy life
Roots grip rock and soil
To counter the earth's imperative spin.
They sleep upright. Stand at attention
Until the wind animates them
Branches grasping air
Like falling children.

Unaware

On the ferry to Crofton
A goat rides in the back of a pickup.
It paces and bleats
Unaware of the journey
It is about to take
Its knowledge
Limited to the farm
It is being moved from.
I catch small glimpses
Of it between pine cross pieces.
Its black head bobs occupied with
Whatever catches such animal's interest.

The goat sniffs the sawdust-laden bed of the truck
And probes with its muzzle for more food.
When the ferry nudges the other shore,
It doesn't look up but goes on eating.
I envy how it lives in the moment
And knows an older time than I do.
Not one measured in days, months or years
But in the span of generations.
Goats don't live in our time
Even though they are amongst us.
Like most animals they have evolved
At a different pace than we have.
Its manners, barnyard manners,
The need to stand its ground
Defend territory.
It has learned as I have
When to push and when to give in.
Its stubbornness visible
In how it continues to hunt

Through the sawdust
Stopping only occasionally to glance
In my direction with widely spaced eyes.

We've used up the earth
Shit where necessary
Believe that every journey leads somewhere.
But they don't always.
Some times we are simply in motion
Headed nowhere.

The truck bearing the goat
Disembarks ahead of me
And I watch the goat steady itself
Against all that jostling.
At the top of the hill
The truck continues north toward Nanaimo
While I turn south toward Duncan
But back there on the ferry
For that briefest of times
We were both
Going to the same place.

Winter Weight

Yesterday a rat died on our front deck
Today maggots have begun to claim its flesh
Death spawning life.
The rat's closed eyes
No longer bothered with this world.
Winter now as distant as the afterlife of rats.
I wonder if heaven has rats
Or do all living creatures simply loop into
Variations of life?

Until the rat died I feared all rats,
But after, I pitied.
I looked at it several times
And wondered exactly
What about it frightened me?
Like me it merely wanted
To sleep each night with a full stomach.
These past weeks it kept us awake
Gnawing in the attic.
During the day it scrounged
Amongst the brush and rubble
Eager to reach its winter weight.

In a week or two
I'll sit out on the deck
Not far from where the rat died
And watch the turned leaves fall.
I could believe that rat
Had its death inside it all along
But I don't. It's the living creatures
I believe in even if in time
They give way to others.

What is next in line
Has always been next in line.
And the earth continues its spin
Clocking the seasons
At a steady, predictable speed.

Liftoff

Yesterday I picked up a hitchhiker
named Jayhawk
He lived in a tent on the beach in Fulford.
He had stuffed his hair into a tam
That hadn't been washed in some time.
He smelled like he hadn't bathed recently.
His worldly possessions were in a black garbage bag.

Before he got out
He asked if I was a store owner
Even though my car was beat up
And I was casually dressed.
Perhaps he thought all store owners
Looked like me.
I took it as a compliment
Even though I told him I wasn't.
He smiled and shook my hand
Then grabbed his bag
From the back seat.
If he traveled any lighter,
He'd liftoff.

As I pulled away
I thought of all those people living
In the bush on Salt Spring Island
Moving mysteriously from camp to camp
When owners get wind
Or just for a change.
They are tolerated here.
I thought too of the homeless people
In Tokyo living in artfully painted
Cardboard boxes all over the city

Many in subway stations.
They too are tolerated.
But for how much longer?
The BC government recently passed a law
Making it illegal to be homeless.
The meek shall never inherit this earth.

Wet Nurse

Cars wait to board
The Long Harbour ferry
Some passengers gather
Outside their vehicles to chat
While others
Listen to music
Or read books
What carries us here
Also carries us away
And once on board the ferry
I look back toward land
Where morning fog has gathered
In low lying pockets
Drawn there by what drew us
The ferry eases out into the harbour
And the drone of its engines
Surges up from beneath the surface
I watch the pier shrink from view
My heart racing toward God knows what.

God Must Have

God must have a God, and that God a God
What is inside of something also has that inside it.
The very large is also the very small.
I discovered that one morning when I saw a snail
Crossing the road where I lived.
In the time I take to drive to Victoria
Or a satellite circles the earth
The snail managed to inch across the road
Without being hit by a car.
His universe is merciful and kind.

Startled

Today I stood on a street corner
And waited for a car to pass
But I sensed that I had
already crossed the road
A thousand times that very moment
And would a thousand times more
Before I actually did.
But what startled me
And caused to me to hold back
Was the realization that
Perhaps what we think of as having a purpose
Is merely the continuous unraveling of what already is.
We are foundlings of the moment
Startled into shape
By forces beyond our knowing or control
It has never been different
Nor will it ever be.

But mostly I stand on street corners
Never certain whether to cross.
Sometimes there is a friend on the other side
Or a shop I want to visit before it closes
But most of the time
Either choice appears the same.
I arrive home at the same time
Carry the same items from the car.
In the house I fill a glass and drink
But the whole time
I feel I am actually somewhere else
In some other house
Drinking from another glass.

After I crossed the street
I spoke with a friend
Both of us making only
Occasional eye contact.
And neither really knew
What the other was saying
When we finally said goodbye
I continued down the little dip
To the grocery store.
Later at the checkout
The clerk took my money
As she has done numerous times before
And slipped my few items into a bag.
All of this too familiar
Not to be happening.

Following the Sound

All month dead wasps
Collected in the trap on our deck.
They continued to enter
Long after the bait had vanished.
I'm not sure what drew them
Except the sounds of those already inside.
Their small bodies formed
A blackened, writhing muck
And each morning I paused
To examine the dying going on inside
And I didn't feel anything and wondered
Why I didn't and then wondered
Why I should?
Sometimes a single survivor
Circled the top eager for a way out.
In a week or two
I will dump the trap
In the garbage
Hiding it beneath other debris.

None of those wasps died
In service of a greater good
Or for love
But some did follow others in.
Finding out too late
How little their lives were worth.

Overlap

The potter at the Fall Fair on Salt Spring
Sat alone in a corner
Ignored by the passing crowd.
Her fingers plied a mauve muck.
As hers hands shaped the clay
It formed smooth curves
That could become anything she wanted.
All shapes start the same.
Rounded lumps. Nothing more.
Then her fingers probed
And the curves became
Harsher, broken almost
No longer curves joining curves, but blunted.
She poked a small mouth at the top
And then pulled out a sharpened hook
Only then did I recognize the spout
And a teapot handle.
She lifted her hands
And let her creation spin slowly.
She reached behind her
To retrieve another lump.
She shifted the fresh clay between her hands
And stopped her potter's wheel
With a knee, then dropped the lump next to
The teapot and gingerly lifted that
And placed it next to several others.

It was at that very moment
That I realized I was witnessing
All creation
Her fingers merely the earth
Reaching out.

Thus is each thing made
And separated from each other
With no overlap
That is what it means to exist
No overlap
Only these grey outlined shapes.

We all came from mud
Our bodies not formed on a potter's wheel
But spun through space
Flesh is made from earth
Not as in the Bible
But worked for a while before
We finally take shape.
Each of us as fluid
As the earth's core.

My Empire of Dirt

The 8 Known Photographs of Arthur Rimbaud

Less than a roll's worth—two taken when he was a boy of eight or ten, two when he was seventeen and already writing. The rest from later when he could be forgiven his weary, defiant gaze.

The earliest is a school photo and his hair is neatly combed and flattened against his head. He sits amongst a group of boys and is not yet the poet we know, but there is evidence of that poet-to-be in his eyes and how they are slightly averted, unlike the other boys who boldly seek the camera's attention. Yet he could be any boy of that time period, one of the first to be photographed, remembered forever in that single stopped moment. In that early picture, it seems likely he is not even thinking of poems, but rather of the next game he will play.

In another he is nearly thirty and wears all white as he poses with a rifle outside an ottoman's pillared residence. He no longer writes poems and soon he will lose a leg to cancer. The photo is clear evidence that poets seldom find that exalted place the poems promise. It's neither poetry's fault nor the poet's.

The final photograph was taken in a garden where he stands alone with arms crossed. Already in his thirties, he resembles an older man, one long finished with love. In those last years he owned a shop in Arden, and only received occasional word of the growing stature of his poems. Soon he would return to France to die.

The photograph of him I love most is the best known, taken when he was seventeen. He has begun to write and is already publishing. From his serious gaze it's clear he is thinking of a poem. The poems came freely then, but not for long, soon he would labour over each one. Words crossed out here and there, replaced by others. As close a notation of his thoughts as we'll ever have. I study those photographs searching for *that* poet, but find only a boy and later an ordinary man.

But the poems at least give him the breathing shape we are after.

The Worth of Fathers
for Bruce Hunter

Your father died yesterday
And I am reminded
Of the worth of fathers.
With our mothers
They have shaped us
Given us time
With which to make yet others.
What breeds us we also breed.
Your father drank and told stories
The liquor loosening the words.
You found in that hard shape of consonants
And vowels a roughly spoken love.

All of us are afforded only
A brief measure of time
And I think of your grief
Where death does not take form
But is the absence of form
Something so unknowable
So unfathomable
That it is
The only certainty.
Where a dead father is only a dead father.
And yet a dead father is everything.

Two of Everything

Noah gathered up the animals
Two at a time.
And created our future.
He lived when God was still everywhere
And paid attention to what we did.

When the waters receded
Noah beached his ark
Threw open the doors
And let the animals run loose
The first ones ventured onto
That muddied, drying world
Seeking a quiet place
To be alone.
Noah and his wife were last
To leave the ark.
Noah went first
So he could assist his wife
Across that wide gap.
In that moment
When he held her
They were finally free of God.

This Shiver

What is this shiver
We rush toward
Until it too is trapped within us
Nothing but a mumbling
Gathered into words.
God is everywhere.
God is *everywhere*,
But here.

Adam's Rib

Why did it start with a rib? Why not a shin, or an elbow, or toe, or finger, or even ear lobe? I suppose it had to be something bountiful, something near the heart, something hidden, something replaceable, something that protects. Why not a lock of hair—that would hardly hurt? Why didn't Eve come first? Why was Adam made out of dust and Eve out of bone? Why weren't they both made from a single breath?

At first, Adam awoke alone to a noisy Eden, his head buzzing with sounds he couldn't name. He felt very lonely as he wandered a place filled with everything but love.

God made Adam out of Eve too and both earned the voices in their heads, the echoes there that God couldn't feed, that made him vanish, even wrong—forgotten for hours at a time. Eve and Adam sat together eating fruit and watching clouds mark the unused sky.

I try to imagine God holding up that curved bone, examining it in the light. Did he already see Eve in his mind or was he expecting someone else? Did he create her in his image or from what Adam could not take in? All the other animals were partnered. Did God plan for Adam to live alone like him? Without Eve, would there have been a purpose to any of it?

Oh God, all your orators speak gibberish

All night a southeast wind blows off the Salish Sea spraying salt water on our windows and deck. Even the arbutus trees that face the ocean are peeled, exposing smooth red skin toward the morning sun. I can't look at them without thinking how time takes everything, leaving nothing behind not even a branch.

Time is in all of us. Even the arbutus out front. Once they were seedlings and later they will be mulch. The earth is a guardian of time, ticking it off in steady beats. All of us, creature, God, plant, and rock come from nothing and return to nothing. We leave stories behind, memories, things others can claim but not for long because they too will vanish.

Even water will not always be water, nor will fire be fire. All that sweet promise, what must we make of it? Time, too, does not want to end.

BOOKS BY ROBERT HILLES

POETRY
Look The Lovely Animal Speaks
The Surprise Element
An Angel In The Works
Outlasting The Landscape
Finding The Lights
On A Breath At A Time
Cantos From A Small Room
Nothing Vanishes
Breathing Distance
Somewhere Between Obstacles and Pleasure
Higher Ground
Wrapped Within Again: New and Selected
Slow Ascent

FICTION
Raising Of Voices
Near Morning
A Gradual Ruin

NON FICTION
Kissing the Smoke
Calling the Wild